RICO TICE | BARRY COOPER

THE REAL JESUS

CHRISTIANITY EXPLORED MINISTRIES

The Real Jesus (3rd Edition)

Reprinted 2018, 2020, 2023.

Published by:
The Good Book Company

thegoodbook COMPANY

thegoodbook.com | thegoodbook.co.uk
thegoodbook.com.au | thegoodbook.co.nz | thegoodbook.co.in

ISBN: 978178498080 | Printed in Turkey by Elma Basim

Design by André Parker

THE REAL **JESUS**

David Hasselhoff is concerned that his role in European history is being overlooked.

In an interview with the *Daily Telegraph*, the actor and singer argued that he helped bring down the Berlin Wall in 1989 by singing "Look For Freedom" on that era-defining night. "I find it a bit sad," said the ex-*Knight Rider* and *Baywatch* star, "that there is no photo of me hanging on the walls in the Berlin Museum".

Is it possible that Jesus had an inflated sense of his own importance too? People were certainly saying some amazing things about him.

> ***Jesus and his disciples went on to the villages around Caesarea Philippi. On the way he asked them, "Who do people say I am?"***
> ***They replied, "Some say John the Baptist; others say Elijah; and still others, one of the prophets."***
> ***"But what about you?" he asked. "Who do you say I am?" Peter answered, "You are the Christ."***
>
> (from the book of Mark in the Bible, chapter 8)

Some people were saying that Jesus was the famous teacher John the Baptist come back from the dead – or even Elijah, one of the great figures of ancient history. There were some who thought that Jesus was "one of the prophets", and even today there are those who would agree.

"But what about you?" says Jesus to his small band of followers. "Who do you say I am?"

Peter, the spokesman of the group, gives his answer: "You are the Christ".

The Real Jesus

Hundreds of years previously, prophets had predicted that the "Christ" would come to rescue those who put their trust in him. He would be born in Bethlehem, they said, come from a particular family line, spend his life in Galilee and teach in parables.

More than that, he would have God's power and authority. As one prophecy put it, "Then the eyes of the blind will be opened and the ears of the deaf unstopped. Then the lame will leap like a deer, and the mute tongue shout for joy" (from Isaiah, chapter 35).

To be fair, having spent nearly three years at his side, Peter had seen Jesus perfectly fulfil these predictions.

He had witnessed Jesus curing crowds of sick people, including the deaf, mute, blind, and paraplegic. He cured them with a simple word or a touch.

He had watched as Jesus easily eclipsed the most brilliant minds of his age, silencing his critics and captivating those who pressed to hear him.

He was travelling in the storm-stricken boat when Jesus had commanded the raging elements to "be still", and they meekly obliged.

He had been present when, on more than one occasion, Jesus had taken the hand of a corpse, and made it live again.

But Peter knew there was more to Jesus even than that. He had never known anyone love as Jesus loved.

Here was a man who embraced the outsider, the downtrodden, the despised, the forgotten – those whom no one else wanted to talk to, let alone love. He treated women with a dignity unusual for his time and welcomed children with open arms.

Here was a man who taught, "Love your enemies and pray for those who persecute you". Later, despite an unjust trial and a brutal execution, he did just that – he prayed for his executioners: "Father, forgive them, for they do not know what they are doing".

After three years of watching Jesus closely, Peter saw no inflated sense of self-importance, even when Jesus said he was "the Son of God", "the Son of Man", "the good shepherd", "the gate", "the way", "the truth", "the resurrection", "the life", "the bread of life", "the true vine" and "the light of the world".

Peter saw nothing strange about Jesus' repeated claims to be God in human form. As far as he could see, they were justified – Jesus really was "the Christ".

Nevertheless, there was something about Jesus that Peter had not yet understood...

The Mission of Jesus

> ***Jesus then began to teach them that the Son of Man must suffer many things and be rejected by the elders, chief priests and teachers of the law, and that he must be killed and after three days rise again.***
>
> (continued from Mark)

Even those who make general statements about their own immediate future often get it wrong, like Margaret Thatcher when she famously said, "I don't think that there will be a woman Prime Minister in my lifetime".

So how many of us could say exactly how we'll die, and who our killers will be, and then correctly predict our return from death three days later?

More than that, Jesus knew that he "must" die. His death had a purpose which had been predicted hundreds of years before he was born. As Isaiah put it, some 700 years previously, "He was pierced for our transgressions, he was crushed for our iniquities; the punishment that brought us peace was upon him, and by his wounds we are healed".

What does Isaiah mean by "our transgressions" and "our iniquities"?

The Most Important Command

According to Jesus, the most important of God's commands is this: "Love the Lord your God with all your heart and with all your soul and with all your mind and with all your strength". God made us, he sustains us, and our response should be to love him – with everything we have.

But none of us have lived like that. As that same prophecy in Isaiah puts it, "We all, like sheep, have gone astray, each of us has turned to his own way..." We live as if we are the centre of the universe, not God.

Jesus explains the reason that we're like this: "For from within, out of men's hearts, come evil thoughts, sexual immorality, theft, murder, adultery, greed, malice, deceit, lewdness, envy, slander, arrogance and folly".

We disregard God's loving laws and we duck his rightful authority over our lives. For whatever reason, we don't trust him to know what's best for us, and we choose to live life as if we're the boss.

And the results of this rebellion are visible all around us: relationships break down, the environment is polluted, communities are blighted by crime, war rages throughout the world and terrorists destroy life as if it did not matter.

Now, to treat another human being as if they don't matter is bad enough, but to treat the Maker of the universe in that way is disastrous.

Because he is good, God will not let evil go unpunished, and treating God in the way we do is the most serious evil of all. It's what the Bible calls "sin".

Jesus is clear that sin results in death – and not just death here, but eternal death, which he describes as "hell". Hell is a place where, for all eternity, people will be punished if they die still rebelling against their Creator. It will be a real place of conscious pain. As you'd expect from the most loving man who ever lived, Jesus takes no pleasure in talking like this. The reason Jesus warns us about hell is because he loves us and does not want us to go there.

The Perfect Substitute

But amazingly, even though we have given up on God, God does not give up on us. Instead, he sent his Son to rescue us by dying for us.

It was a death that had been predicted hundreds of years earlier, in remarkable detail: he would be rejected by his own people; he would be falsely accused but refuse to retaliate or speak up in his own defence; he would be mocked and brutally beaten (although not one of his bones would be broken); he would be executed with criminals, with spectators jeering at him and challenging God to rescue him; his killers would decide who would get his clothes by gambling for them.

In all, twenty-nine such prophecies were fulfilled in the final twenty-four hours of Jesus' life, as he was tried, condemned and then executed on a Roman cross.

So there was nothing accidental about Jesus' death. There was nothing pointless about it either.

As he died, crying out, "My God, my God, why have you forsaken me?" Jesus was enduring the separation from God that each one of us deserves for our rebellion. He was enduring it on our behalf. He went through it so that we never have to, if only we will trust him.

That's why Jesus said that he "must" die.

Jesus died willingly so that we could be reconciled with our Creator. He died as our substitute, in our place, taking the punishment we deserve.

The Loving Ransom

In the United States, there is a gravestone with a simple inscription on it. It says this: "I want to stand where you're standing". Underneath those words is the lovingly engraved story of an incident that occurred during the American Civil War.

A soldier, only 19 years of age, was part of a firing squad assigned to execute a man guilty of treason. As he closed one eye and took aim down the barrel of his gun, he was horrified to see that he knew the man he was about to shoot. He lowered his gun, walked over to his captain, and said, "I can't do it. That man has a wife and children at home. If I shoot him, I not only end his life, but I end their lives too. I will make his wife a widow and I'll be robbing the children of their father. I can't do it."

But everyone knew that the punishment for treason was death. The price had to be paid.

So after a short discussion, they came up with a plan. They agreed that the young soldier could take the condemned man's place. The 19-year-old marched up to the captive and said simply, "I want to stand where you're standing".

The captive took off his blindfold, and walked away. Back to his wife, his family, his life. But his freedom came at great cost to another: the young man who had chosen to die in his place.

That is just a small glimpse of what Jesus achieved on the cross. As he went willingly to his death, it was as if he was saying to each one of us, "I want to stand where you're standing". And his death earned the freedom of more than one person. He died – to use the words he used himself – "as a ransom for many".

The Great Escape

And when he rose from death three days later, just as he'd promised he would, Jesus proved that death had no power over him – or those who follow him.

His resurrection offers those who follow him certainty and hope in the face of death: "My sheep listen to my voice; I know them, and they follow me. I give them eternal life, and they shall never perish."

This "eternal life" that Jesus offers is just as real and physical as the life we are living now, but with one important difference – there will be no more sin.

And the implications of that are staggering: no more suffering, no more disease, no more fear, no more regrets, no more loneliness, no more unfulfilled dreams, no more death. Jesus promises those who follow him that they will "have life, and have it to the full".

The Cost of Following Jesus

> ***Then he called the crowd to him along with his disciples and said: "If anyone would come after me, he must deny himself and take up his cross and follow me. For whoever wants to save his life will lose it, but whoever loses his life for me and for the gospel will save it. What good is it for a man to gain the whole world, yet lose his soul?"***
>
> (continued from Mark)

If we choose to follow Christ, we have everything to gain: "whoever loses his life for me and for the gospel will save it".

Jesus tells us elsewhere that his Spirit will come to live in us, we'll be forgiven, we'll enjoy a deep sense of peace, joy, purpose and freedom, and we'll know for certain that we have eternal life.

We were made to be in this relationship with our Creator, and without it we are bound to feel as if something is missing. With that relationship in place, however, we can finally begin to live as we were meant to live.

But, if we choose to follow Christ, we also have much to lose: "If anyone would come after me, he must deny himself and take up his cross and follow me".

Following Jesus means "denying self": it means turning away from selfish instincts, living for God – and for others – rather than for ourselves. It means being for what Jesus is for, and against what Jesus is against.

Following Jesus also means "taking up our cross": it means being prepared to suffer and face opposition for his sake.

Living like that may cost us dearly in terms of our friends, family, popularity, wealth and career. But, as Jesus reminds us, what is the point of having all those things if they cost us the most valuable thing we have? "What good is it for a man to gain the whole world," says Jesus, "yet lose his soul?"

And if – by the same token – you suffer for following Christ, what does it matter? You still have the most precious thing in the world, bar none: the pleasure of knowing God, and his forgiveness.

The following exchange recently appeared on the internet, claiming to be a transcript of a radio conversation that actually happened, although the story was immediately denied by the US authorities.

Ship: Please divert your course 0.5 degrees to the south to avoid a collision.

Reply: Recommend you divert your course 15 degrees to the south to avoid a collision.

Ship: This is the captain of a US Navy ship. I say again, divert your course.

Reply: No. I say again, you divert YOUR course!

Ship: THIS IS THE AIRCRAFT CARRIER USS CORAL SEA. WE ARE A LARGE WARSHIP OF THE US NAVY. DIVERT YOUR COURSE NOW!

Reply: This is a lighthouse. Your call.

People respond to Jesus in lots of different ways. Some choose to ignore him, some deliberately reject him, and some try to put off the decision until later.

But Jesus – this man of unmatched power, authority, integrity and love – reminds us that the consequences of such a choice are out of our hands: "Whoever wants to save his life will lose it, but whoever loses his life for me and for the gospel will save it."

Your call.

What next?

Now that you've read this booklet, you might like to:

Pray. If you want to start following Jesus, you could use the prayer below to mark the beginning of your Christian life:

> ***Lord God, I am so sorry that I have not loved you with all my heart, soul, mind and strength.***
>
> ***I understand now who Jesus is and why he died. I know that I do not deserve it, but because of Jesus' death on a cross for me, I ask you to forgive me.***
>
> ***From now on, please give me the desire to obey you, and help me to follow Jesus – whatever the cost.***

If you said this prayer, it's a good idea to tell another Christian as soon as possible so that they can offer you support. You are about to explore an amazing new life!

Join a Course. If you still have questions, why not join a *Christianity Explored* or *Life Explored* course? It's informal and relaxed. You won't be asked to read aloud, pray or sing. You can ask any question you like – or you can just sit and listen. Visit www.christianityexplored.org, click "What's Next", and scroll down to "Find a Church or Course Near You".

THE REAL
JESUS

- Teacher...
- Healer...
- Prophet...
- Revolutionary...
- Miracle-worker...

Who is the real Jesus?

ISBN 978-1-78498-080-1

9 781784 980801

CHRISTIANITY EXPLORED MINISTRIES

thegoodbook COMPANY